Art Styles

Graffiti

by Julie Murray

Dash!
LEVELED READERS
An Imprint of Abdo Zoom • abdobooks.com

Dash!
LEVELED READERS

Level 1 – Beginning
Short and simple sentences with familiar words or patterns for children who are beginning to understand how letters and sounds go together.

Level 2 – Emerging
Longer words and sentences with more complex language patterns for readers who are practicing common words and letter sounds.

Level 3 – Transitional
More developed language and vocabulary for readers who are becoming more independent.

THIS BOOK CONTAINS RECYCLED MATERIALS

abdobooks.com

Published by Abdo Zoom, a division of ABDO, PO Box 398166, Minneapolis, Minnesota 55439.

Printed in the United States of America, North Mankato, Minnesota.
102023
012024

Photo Credits: Getty Images, Shutterstock
Production Contributors: Kenny Abdo, Jennie Forsberg, Grace Hansen, John Hansen
Design Contributors: Candice Keimig, Neil Klinepier

Library of Congress Control Number: 2023937915

Publisher's Cataloging in Publication Data

Names: Murray, Julie, author.
Title: Graffiti / by Julie Murray
Description: Minneapolis, Minnesota : Abdo Zoom, 2024 | Series: Art styles | Includes online resources and index.
Identifiers: ISBN 9781098283940 (lib. bdg.) | ISBN 9781098284664 (eBook) | ISBN 9781098285029 (Read-to-Me eBook)
Subjects: LCSH: Graffiti--Juvenile literature. | Street art--Juvenile literature. | Mural painting and decoration--Juvenile literature. | Wall-painting--Juvenile literature.
Classification: DDC 751.73--dc23

Table of Contents

Graffiti

Graffiti is an art style that uses symbols, words, or pictures. It is done on a public surface, often without permission. Some see graffiti as a form of **self-expression**.

History

Graffiti has been around for thousands of years. Early civilizations carved and painted images on cave walls. Ancient Romans and Greeks wrote words and drew pictures on buildings.

Modern graffiti began in Philadelphia in the 1960s. It became popular in New York City in the 1970s. Graffiti appeared on subways, trains, and buildings all over the city.

SPY-161

Famous street artists, such as Banksy, use graffiti to make political and social **commentary**. Banksy's art appears on public surfaces throughout the world.

Kinds of Graffiti

Tagging is the simplest form of graffiti. It is the artist's signature. Spray paint is commonly used for tagging. Often, just one color is used.

A throw-up or "throwie" is more involved and larger in size. The letters are often done in bubble-style using two colors.

Stencils can be used to create an image or text. Paint transfers the shapes to a surface. Banksy uses this style of graffiti art.

17

KOBRA
KOBRA

Famous **muralist** Eduardo Kobra began his career in graffiti. Today, Kobra is asked to paint his street art on buildings around the world.

Graffiti has become an **urban** art form. Some cities have **designated** areas for artists to display their work. It is quickly becoming a popular art style!

More Facts

- A "piece" is a graffiti masterpiece. It is large, complex, and painted freehand. More than three colors are used in this kind of graffiti.
- Darryl McCray is known as the first modern graffiti artist. He goes by the name Cornbread.
- Graffiti is illegal when put on property without permission. The US spends more than $12 billion a year cleaning up graffiti.

Glossary

commentary – something that serves as an example.

designated – chosen for a particular purpose.

muralist – an artist who paints murals. A mural is a large picture painted on a wall or ceiling.

self-expression – the expression of one's feelings, thoughts, or ideas, especially in writing, art, music, or dance.

urban – of or having to do with a city or town.

Index

Online Resources

To learn more about graffiti, please visit **abdobooklinks.com** or scan this QR code. These links are routinely monitored and updated to provide the most current information available.